Bill Clinton

History Maker Bios

Stephanie Sammartino McPherson

BARNES & NOBLE

NEW YORK

Text © 2008 by Stephanie Sammartino McPherson
Illustrations © 2008 by Lerner Publishing Group, Inc.

This 2008 edition published by Barnes & Noble, Inc.
by arrangement with Lerner Publications Company, a division of
Lerner Publishing Group, Inc., Minneapolis, MN.

Illustrations by Tad Butler

ISBN-13: 978-1-4351-0164-7
ISBN-10: 1-4351-0164-2

Printed and bound in the United States of America

1 3 5 7 9 10 8 6 4 2

Table of Contents

INTRODUCTION

Bill Clinton liked to dream big. As a young man, he wanted to run for Congress. He wanted to make life better for all Americans. It wouldn't be easy. But Bill believed in himself and in his country. He could talk to an important politician as easily as he talked to an ordinary voter. And he cared deeply about the issues.

People began to take notice of Bill. He never got to Congress. But when he was only thirty-two years old, the people of Arkansas elected him governor. In 1992, he became the third-youngest person to be elected president of the United States. Bill worked hard for civil rights, gun control, health care, and world peace. No matter what happened, he refused to give up.

This is his story.

1 A Passion
for Justice

August 19, 1946, was both a happy and a sad day for Virginia Blythe. She was happy because her son William Jefferson Blythe IV was born. She was sad because her husband, William III, had died three months earlier in a car crash. Virginia's baby, nicknamed Billy, would never know his father.

But Billy grew up surrounded by love. He lived with his mother and her parents in Hope, Arkansas. They made Billy feel protected and special.

Billy's mother was a nurse. When he was one year old, she went to New Orleans for extra training. This would help her get a better job. Billy stayed with Mammaw and Pawpaw, as he called his grandparents.

Mammaw wanted Billy to be healthy and smart. She made alphabet cards and number cards. She stuck them to the window by Billy's high chair. The cards helped him learn to read and count at an early age.

As a young child, Billy had curly hair and a bright smile.

Pawpaw stands at the counter of his grocery store.

Pawpaw ran a grocery store. Billy often went to work with him. Many of the customers were African Americans. In the South, African Americans and whites went to different restaurants and schools. They did not live in the same neighborhoods or attend the same churches. Pawpaw knew this was wrong. He treated his black customers exactly as he treated his white customers. Billy made friends with black children in the store. He grew up respecting people of all races.

In June 1950, Billy's mother returned to Hope. She married a man named Roger Clinton. He owned a car dealership. Roger wanted to be a good father to Billy. But Roger had a drinking problem. Sometimes he became violent. Once Billy saw him fire a gun in anger. Billy was terrified.

After first grade, Billy moved with his family to the small city of Hot Springs, Arkansas. Billy was a friendly, talkative boy. He had a thick mop of curly hair. Despite problems at home, he did well in school. And he loved playing saxophone in the school band.

Billy poses at home with his saxophone.

When Bill was ten years old, his mother had a baby boy. She named him Roger. Bill was a proud big brother and a caring son. As Bill and young Roger grew older, their father's violence grew worse. Bill stood up for his mother. He ordered Roger Clinton to leave her alone. Finally, in 1962, Virginia divorced her husband. Bill knew the divorce was hard on his brother. He didn't want young Roger to feel alone. Bill changed his own name from Blythe to Clinton. This way, both brothers would have the same last name.

Bill stands with his little brother and dog in front of his family home in 1962.

To Bill's surprise, his mother decided to remarry Roger. Bill was worried. But when Roger Clinton wasn't drinking, he could be interesting and kind.

Bill never told his friends about the problems in his home life. He eagerly took part in lots of school activities. After his junior year in high school, he spent one week at Arkansas Boys State. This was a special program for boys that let them take part in a mock, or pretend, state government. The boys discussed important issues. They held elections. Bill was elected to be one of the two boy senators from the state of Arkansas. That meant he would attend Boys Nation in Washington, D.C.

At Boys Nation, Bill went to a mock Congress. He had a passion for justice. He told everyone that people of all races should have the same rights. Bill enjoyed seeing the city and visiting the U.S. Capitol. The boys went to the White House. Bill was thrilled when President John Kennedy stepped out of his office to join the boys on the lawn. Bill got to shake hands with his hero! By the time school started that fall, Bill was sure he wanted a career in politics.

Bill shakes hands with President Kennedy during the Boys Nation visit to the White House.

EVERYTHING BILL BELIEVED

About one month after meeting President John Kennedy, Bill watched another of his heroes on television. Martin Luther King Jr. made one of the most important speeches in U.S. history. He told the country about his great dream. King believed that one day people of all races would live together in friendship. "I started crying during the speech," Bill wrote years later. "He had said everything I believe."

2 AMBITIOUS PROFESSOR

After high school, Bill decided to go to Georgetown University in Washington, D.C. He also got a job as a clerk for Senator William Fulbright of Arkansas. That meant Bill carried important papers back and forth between the senator's office and the Capitol. He kept track of the senator's mailing list. Sometimes Bill became so tired that he fell asleep on the job. But he loved working for Senator Fulbright.

Bill met many people in the senator's office. He talked with some of them about ending a war that was raging in Vietnam. President Lyndon Johnson had sent U.S. troops to fight in that country. He feared that the nation would become Communist. Communists did not believe in the U.S. system of government. They did not allow freedom of speech or religion. Some Americans were afraid that Communists were trying to take over the world. So they wanted to stop Communists in Vietnam.

Bill posed for this yearbook picture during his first year at Georgetown University.

Senator Fulbright was against the war. Like many people, he believed it was wrong to send U.S. soldiers to fight and die in Vietnam. In the senator's office, Bill saw a daily list of men from Arkansas who had died in the war. He felt terrible when he saw the name of a schoolmate on the list.

Bill knew that his own future was uncertain. After graduation from Georgetown in 1968, he won a Rhodes scholarship. Rhodes scholarships allow students to study at Oxford University in England for two years.

WORKING HARDER

As Bill's senior year approached, he decided to run for student body president. He already knew about school politics. He had been president of the freshman and sophomore classes. But to his disappointment, Bill did not win the election. "If I [run] again, I'll just have to work harder," he said.

Bill sits on a wall overlooking the Thames River in Oxford.

Bill knew he could be drafted before that time was over. If he was drafted, he would be forced to join the military. He could be sent to fight in Vietnam even though he did not believe in the war. But Bill did not get drafted. Instead, he spent two years studying in England.

When Bill returned to the United States, he went to law school at Yale University. One young woman there captured Bill's attention. The young woman noticed Bill too. Finally, she approached him. "We ought to at least know each other's names," she said. "Mine's Hillary Rodham."

Bill and Hillary met at Yale University in New Haven, Connecticut. This picture was taken at the Yale Law School in 1972.

Later, Bill met Hillary on her way to sign up for the next term's classes. Bill's classes were all set. But he pretended he had to register too. Hillary laughed when she discovered his trick. Soon, they were spending lots of time together. After only one month, Bill knew that he loved Hillary.

Hillary was as interested in politics as Bill was. The year 1972 marked a presidential election. Democrat George McGovern was running against Republican president Richard Nixon. Both Bill and Hillary agreed with McGovern that the war in Vietnam should end.

That summer, Bill worked for the McGovern campaign at the Democratic National Convention in Florida. After McGovern won the nomination, Bill went to Texas. Democratic officials wanted someone from out of state to take charge of the campaign in Texas. They thought that Bill could do that. Hillary joined the campaign in Texas several weeks later.

Bill worked for McGovern until the November election. He was disappointed but not surprised when President Nixon won. Bill returned to law school two months after the term had started. "Aren't you worried about classes?" someone asked him. But Bill wasn't worried. He studied hard for his finals and passed all his classes.

George McGovern (LEFT) greets his supporters.

After Bill graduated from Yale, he went back to Arkansas. He became a law professor at the University of Arkansas in Fayetteville. Bill was a popular teacher. Students liked the lively discussions he led. African American students were especially glad for his friendship. Many had attended segregated schools. Some of these schools were not as good as the schools white children had attended. Most of the African American students were not well prepared for law school. Bill cared about their success. He helped many of them with their studies.

Bill enjoyed teaching. But soon, his thoughts turned to politics. On February 25, 1974, he announced that he was running for Congress.

A sign supporting Bill's run for Congress hangs outside an Arkansas home.

Bill drove all over the Arkansas countryside to meet voters. He loved talking to folks in restaurants, stores, and gas stations. Many people agreed with Bill's ideas. They liked his enthusiasm. But he did not win. Luckily, Hillary had moved to Arkansas by then. She taught at the same school as Bill. With Hillary's help, he got over his disappointment. He was not giving up on politics.

3 THE YOUNGEST GOVERNOR

Bill had asked Hillary to marry him several times. But she couldn't make up her mind. Then Bill secretly bought a house that Hillary had seen and liked. "You have to marry me now, because I can't live there alone," he said. At last, Hillary said yes! Bill and Hillary were married in the house on October 11, 1975.

As attorney general, Bill acted as the lawyer for the State of Arkansas.

The next year, Bill was elected attorney general of Arkansas. His political career had finally begun! Bill and Hillary left their house in Fayetteville and moved to the capital city of Little Rock. Bill worked with the lawmakers on important issues. Were people in nursing homes receiving the best care? Were there ways to keep the cost of gas and electricity from rising? These were some of the concerns that kept Bill Clinton busy.

Hillary watches as Bill swears to serve responsibly as the governor of Arkansas.

People from all parts of the state knew and respected Bill. In 1978, they elected him governor of Arkansas. Thirty-two-year-old Bill was the youngest governor in the nation. He worked hard to improve schools and roads. He sought ways to save energy and to protect natural resources. But Bill's happiest moment came when his daughter, Chelsea, was born on February 27, 1980. Later, he wrote that he "knew . . . being a father was the most important job [he'd] ever have."

Bill and Hillary hold newborn Chelsea.

Bill had done good things for Arkansas. But he also made some mistakes. Many people were angry because he raised the taxes on cars. They voted not to return him to office. The election results were a big disappointment to Bill. He missed the excitement of politics. He said he felt like "a fish out of water."

Bill did not stay down for long. On Chelsea's second birthday, he made it official. He would seek another term as governor. This time, he was successful. No other Arkansas governor had ever regained the office after losing an earlier race for reelection.

Hillary (STANDING, AT RIGHT) visits an Arkansas kindergarten class. She worked to help children learn to read.

Bill had big plans to improve education in Arkansas. The state was known for its poor schools. Bill formed a committee to study the problem. He asked Hillary to be in charge of it. Bill and members of the committee wanted smaller classes and more pay for teachers. They called for more math and science courses. And they wanted teachers to take tests to make sure they were qualified. The state legislature passed laws to make these changes.

People in other states began to notice Bill. In 1986, when he was forty years old, he became the chairman of the National Governors Association (NGA). He liked to talk about education, the need for more jobs, and better ways to help poor people. Soon, organizations all over the country were asking Bill to come and speak to them. Some Democrats began to think he should run for president.

Bill speaks to the National Governors Association. He met many important politicians while he led that association.

In 1990, Bill gave an important speech to the Democratic Leadership Council. This group had been organized to show Americans that Democrats had good ideas. Their views on money, national defense, and other issues could make the nation stronger. But many people worried about the Democratic Party. The Republicans were winning more elections.

Bill wanted to do more than save the Democratic Party. "We are here to save the United States of America," he declared. He wanted all citizens to take part in the government. Bill's speech impressed reporters and politicians. They thought he would be a strong candidate to run against

President George Herbert Walker Bush.

Bill addresses the Democratic Leadership Council in 1991. He led the group from 1990 to 1991.

After ten years as governor, Bill was ready to move on. Chelsea and Hillary stood beside him on October 3, 1991, as he declared that he would run for president.

THE COMEBACK KID

When he was seeking the nomination for president, Bill had to enter state primaries. In primaries, members of a political party choose their party's presidential candidate. Bill was doing poorly in the primaries. It looked as if he might not get to run for president after all. Then he did well in the New Hampshire primary. That put him back in the race. Bill gave himself a nickname—the comeback kid. He was to have many more ups and downs in his career.

4 A TROUBLED PRESIDENCY

After the Democrats nominated him for president in July 1992, Bill set off on a campaign bus tour with Hillary. Vice-presidential candidate Al Gore and his wife, Tipper, went with them. Bill enjoyed meeting people and shaking hands with the voters. Sometimes he saw groups of people waving from the side of the road. Bill would call for the bus to stop so he could talk to them.

Usually a presidential race is between two candidates. But Bill had two opponents to beat. President George H. W. Bush was running for reelection. And businessperson Ross Perot was challenging both the Republicans and the Democrats. He was running as a third-party candidate.

On Election Day, twelve-year-old Chelsea went to the polls with her dad. He let her push the lever beside his name. (On some voting machines, a lever is beside each candidate's name. Voters push the lever next to their favorite candidate.) Then she gave him a big hug.

Bill (RIGHT) compares his political views with President Bush (LEFT) and Ross Perot (MIDDLE) at a debate.

Bill, Hillary, and Chelsea spent the rest of the day at the governor's mansion. They watched the election news on TV. Late that night, reporters proclaimed Bill president-elect of the United States. That meant he had won the election! But he wouldn't officially become president until he took the oath of office in January.

Bill and Hillary wave to supporters after the announcement of Bill's victory in the election.

Bill takes the president's oath of office in a ceremony held in front of the U.S. Capitol Building.

On January 16, 1993, Bill took the oath of office in front of the U.S. Capitol. Then he gave his first speech as president. Bill was honest about the problems Americans faced. Some people didn't make enough money. Others couldn't find jobs. The cost of health care was high. But Bill believed in the future. "There is nothing wrong with America that can't be cured by what is right with America," he said.

Bill spent the next four years trying to make life better for ordinary citizens. He created new jobs and lowered taxes for poor people. He signed a law that put more police officers on the streets. He also supported the Brady law. This law made it harder for people to buy guns. Bill believed that fewer guns would help lower the crime rate.

What could young people do for the country? Bill had an answer for that question too. He started AmeriCorps. This organization gives many people a chance to help others. They could do many jobs, such as clean parks, build homes, or teach people to read and write.

Bill listens as new members of AmeriCorps pledge to work for a safer and healthier United States.

FREE EXCHANGE OF GOODS

On December 8, 1993, Bill signed the North Atlantic Free Trade Agreement, or NAFTA. This made it easier for countries in North America to exchange goods with one another. Bill hoped the agreement would help business and create new jobs in the United States.

But sometimes personal problems took Bill's mind off his job. Years earlier, Bill and his wife had bought land in Arkansas. They thought that the land would become more valuable. But later, their business partners were accused of wrongdoing. Some people questioned Bill's honesty too.

Bill appointed a lawyer to look into the matter. The lawyer would investigate the charges. This was a big step. But Bill wasn't worried. He knew that he had not done anything wrong.

The public didn't seem worried either. Bill was a very popular president. Americans liked the way he was running the country. They liked his friendliness and warmth. In 1996, Bill easily won reelection, defeating Republican Bob Dole.

But Bill's troubles were not over. The lawyer, a man named Kenneth Starr, began to look into Bill's personal life. He called Bill to explain his relationship with a young woman who had worked at the White House. Her name was Monica Lewinsky. Starr believed that Bill may have had a personal relationship with Monica. And Bill was not supposed to have personal relationships with people who worked for him.

Monica Lewinsky stands next to Bill at a presidential campaign event in 1996.

Bill said he hadn't done anything wrong. But Kenneth Starr kept studying the matter. Newspapers made the issue a top story. Bill was forced to admit that he had lied about the relationship. Republicans began to call for his impeachment because he lied under oath. To be impeached is to be removed from public office.

A president can be removed from office only if he is found guilty of committing a serious crime. Both houses of Congress are involved in the impeachment process. First, the House of Representatives has to vote for impeachment. This means they believe there is evidence of a serious crime. Then the Senate holds a trial. If the senators find the president guilty, he is removed from office.

People were sharply divided over what Bill should do. He could resign to spare the country the difficulty of an impeachment. Or he could fight.

Bill knew he had made a serious mistake. But he was determined not to let it destroy his presidency. He decided to fight.

5 HOPE FOR THE FUTURE

In December 1998, the House of Representatives voted to impeach Bill. Moments afterward, Vice President Al Gore led a group of Democrats on a march to the White House. They wanted to show their support for Bill. Less than two months later, the Senate found Bill not guilty. He could finish the rest of his term.

U.S. senators vote on whether to remove Bill from office.

Bill was grateful that he was not removed from office. He told the American people how sorry he was for what he had done. For two more years, he pushed for laws to protect the environment and to fight crime. And he continued to do whatever he could to bring peace to the world. Hillary helped too. She soon decided that she wanted to run for the Senate. That way, she could help her country even more. Bill supported her all the way. They bought an old farmhouse in Chappaqua, New York. The next month, Hillary announced her candidacy.

Hillary and Vice President Al Gore reenact her oath of office. Bill and Chelsea stand to the left.

To Bill's delight, Hillary won her race for the Senate. On January 3, 2001, he attended her swearing-in ceremony with Chelsea. "I was so excited I nearly jumped over the railing," he recalled.

Seventeen days later, Bill left the presidency. At fifty-four, he was energetic and full of plans. He set up an office in the Harlem section of New York City. He started an organization called the Bill Clinton Foundation. It works to help poor people. And it tries to help people of different races get along. Bill also wanted to fight AIDS. He encouraged governments to develop programs to help AIDS patients.

IN TIMES OF HARDSHIP

Like all Americans, Bill was shocked when the World Trade Center was destroyed on September 11, 2001. He wanted to help the families of the victims. He teamed up with Bob Dole, the man he had defeated for president. Together they raised money for children who had lost a parent in the attack. Several years later, Bill worked with the other man he had defeated—George Herbert Walker Bush. A tsunami, or tidal wave, had crashed into countries on the Indian Ocean. The two former presidents raised money to help the countries rebuild. In 2005, they also raised money for the victims of Hurricane Katrina.

For three years, Bill was on the go. He traveled throughout the United States. He visited fifty-four countries. Then, in 2004, he was diagnosed with heart disease.

Doctors performed surgery. After he recovered, Bill made changes in the way he ate. He started to eat foods low in fat. He lost weight. Then he worked to teach children proper eating habits. He wanted to help them lead healthy lives.

Nothing was going to slow Bill down. He continued to travel all over the world. He wrote books and made speeches. Most of the money from his speeches went to his foundation to help others.

Bill (LEFT) and former president George H.W. Bush (RIGHT) visit children left homeless by a tsunami in Sri Lanka in 2004.

Hillary speaks to Democratic Party members in Iowa in 2007.

Politics continues to play a big role in Bill's life. During Hillary's second term as senator, she announced that she was running for president. She wanted to win the 2008 election. Bill believes she would make an excellent president. He does everything he can to help her win the nomination of the Democratic Party.

Whatever happens, Bill will surely keep busy. "I have had a wonderful life," he told a news reporter. "I think I owe it to . . . people throughout the world to spend time saving lives, solving problems [and] helping people see the future."

TIMELINE

BILL CLINTON
WAS BORN ON
AUGUST 19, 1946.

In the year . . .

1953 Bill's family moved to Hot Springs, Arkansas.

1963 he went to Boys Nation and met President John Kennedy. | Age 16 |

1968 Bill graduated from Georgetown University. he went to England as a Rhodes scholar.

1973 he graduated from Yale Law School.

1975 he married Hillary Rodham on October 11.

1976 he was elected attorney general of Arkansas.

1978 he was elected governor of Arkansas. | Age 32 |

1980 daughter, Chelsea, was born on February 27. he lost his bid for reelection.

1982 he regained the governorship.

1986 he became chairman of the National Governors Association.

1992 he was elected president of the United States.

1993 he founded AmeriCorps. | Age 46 |

1993 he signed the Brady law. he signed the North Atlantic Free Trade Agreement (NAFTA).

1996 he was reelected president.

1998 the House of Representatives voted to impeach him in December.

1999 the Senate voted not to remove him from office.

2004 he underwent heart surgery.

2005 he established the Clinton Global Initiative to fight poverty worldwide. | Age 59 |

2008 he campaigned for Hillary's presidential race.

CLINTON GLOBAL INITIATIVE

Bill Clinton believes that people of all nations should help one another. In 2005, he invited citizens from many countries to take part in his Clinton Global Initiative. (An initiative is a first step in trying to solve a problem.) This was a worldwide call to action.

Government officials, scientists, businesspeople, and religious leaders all came together. Bill wanted them to think about problems and find ways to solve them. He asked the gathering to especially think about four things:
- how to end poverty
- how to increase understanding among all religions
- how to protect the planet
- how to help new democracies

According to Bill, the Clinton Global Initiative "is making a difference by matching good ideas with the people who can . . . [make them happen]." He feels the initiative will help shape a better future for everyone.

Bill speaks at a Clinton Global Initiative meeting.

CLINTON GLOBAL INITIATIVE

FURTHER READING

Landau, Elaine. *The President's Work.* Minneapolis: Lerner Publications Company, 2004. This book takes a look at the various roles of a U.S. president.

Marcovitz, Hal. *Bill Clinton.* Broomall, PA: Mason Crest Publishers, 2002. Part of the Childhoods of the Presidents series, this book sticks to the main facts of Bill's childhood but imagines some of the details.

O'Shei, Tim. *Bill Clinton.* Berkeley Heights, NJ: Enslow, 2003. This book has a link to a website.

Sutcliffe, Jane. *John F. Kennedy.* Minneapolis: Lerner Publications Company, 2005. This book tells the life story of President Kennedy, one of Clinton's childhood heroes.

WEBSITES

Biography of William J. Clinton
http://www.whitehouse.gov/history/presidents/bc42.html
This site provides a brief look at Bill's life and a link to presidential biographies done by kids.

William J. Clinton Foundation
http://www.clintonfoundation.org/
This site describes the activities of the Clinton Foundation and tells about the Clinton Global Initiative.

SELECT BIBLIOGRAPHY

Bernstein, Carl. *A Woman in Charge: The Life of Hillary Rodham Clinton*. New York: Alfred A. Knopf, 2007.

Clinton, Bill. *My Life*. New York: Vintage Books, 2005.

Clinton, Hillary Rodham. *Living History*. New York: Scribner, 2003.

Darman, Jonathan. "His New Role." *Newsweek*, May 28, 2007.

Hamilton, Nigel. *Bill Clinton: Mastering the Presidency*. New York: Public Affairs, 2007.

Harris, John F. *The Survivor: Bill Clinton in the White House*. New York: Random House Trade Paperback, 2006.

Klein, Joe. *The Natural: The Misunderstood Presidency of Bill Clinton*. New York: Broadway Books, 2002.

Maraniss, David. *First in His Class: The Biography of Bill Clinton*. New York: A Touchstone Book, 1995.

Milton, Joyce. *The First Partner: Hillary Rodham Clinton: A Biography*. New York: Perennial, 1999.

Pearson Education. "William Jefferson Clinton." *Infoplease*.com. May 29, 2007. http://www.infoplease.com/ipa/A0760626.html (February 18, 1008).

Sigall, Edward. "Bill Clinton Still (very much) In Power." *Newsmax*, November 2007.

INDEX

Acknowledgments

The images in this book are used with the permission of: © Jason Kempin/ FilmMagic/Getty Images, p. 4; © Getty Images, p. 7; William J. Clinton Foundation, p. 8; William J. Clinton Presidential Library, pp. 9, 10, 17, 18, 23, 25, 33, 34, 40; © Art Meripol/Sygma/CORBIS, p. 11; © JFK Collection/ZUMA Press, p. 12; Georgetown University Library Special Collections, p. 15; Independent Picture Service, p. 19; © Hot Springs High School/ZUMA Press, p. 20; Arkansas Democrat-Gazette, pp. 24, 26; © Bettmann/CORBIS, p. 27; © Bill Swersey/Liaison/ Getty Images, p. 28; © Wally McNamee/CORBIS, p. 31; © Kelly Quinn, p. 32; Anonymous, p. 36; © AFP/Getty Images, p. 39; AP Photo/Gerald Herbert, p. 42; © Scott Olson/Getty Images, p. 43; © Chris Hondros/Getty Images, p. 45.

Front cover: William J. Clinton Presidential Library
Back cover: © Todd Strand/Independent Pictures Service

Bill Clinton

Stephanie Sammartino McPherson